MEDIA MATTERS
THEN AND NOW

Abdo & Daughters
MIDDLE GRADE NONFICTION

An imprint of Abdo Publishing
abdobooks.com

Rachael L. Thomas

ABDOBOOKS.COM

Published by Abdo Publishing, a division of ABDO, PO Box 398166, Minneapolis, Minnesota 55439. Copyright © 2022 by Abdo Consulting Group, Inc. International copyrights reserved in all countries. No part of this book may be reproduced in any form without written permission from the publisher. Abdo & Daughters™ is a trademark and logo of Abdo Publishing.

Printed in the United States of America, North Mankato, Minnesota

052021

092021

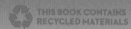
THIS BOOK CONTAINS RECYCLED MATERIALS

Design: Kelly Doudna, Mighty Media, Inc.

Production: Mighty Media, Inc.

Editor: Jessica Rusick

Cover Photographs: AP Images (left); Michael Brochstein/AP Images

Interior Photographs: adoc-photos/Getty Images, p. 13 (bottom); AP Images, p. 1 (left); California Digital Newspaper Collection, p. 7; CDC, pp. 33, 45; The Crowley Company/Library of Congress, pp. 8, 44; DM/AP Images, p. 24; Ed Uthman/Flickr, p. 9; Jim West/Alamy, pp. 4–5; Juan Karita/AP Images, p. 36; Kin Cheung/AP Images, p. 29 (bottom); Library of Congress, pp. 12, 15, 19; Maryland GovPics/Flickr, p. 30; Michael Brochstein/AP Images, p. 1; Nathan Denette/AP Images, pp. 26–27; National Archives and Records Administration, pp. 10–11, 13, 14, 20; NIH/Flickr, p. 28; Senate Democrats/Flickr, p. 37; Shutterstock Images, pp. 16, 21, 22–23, 29, 31, 34–35, 39, 40, 41, 42; The White House/Flickr, p. 6; Wikimedia Commons, pp. 17, 18

Design Elements: Shutterstock Images

LIBRARY OF CONGRESS CONTROL NUMBER: 2020949729

PUBLISHER'S CATALOGING-IN-PUBLICATION DATA

Names: Thomas, Rachael L., author.

Title: Media matters: then and now / by Rachael L. Thomas

Other title: then and now

Description: Minneapolis, Minnesota : Abdo Publishing, 2022 | Series: Pandemics | Includes online resources and index

Identifiers: ISBN 9781532195594 (lib. bdg.) | ISBN 9781098216320 (ebook)

Subjects: LCSH: History in mass media--Juvenile literature. | Social sciences in mass media--Juvenile literature. | Rumor in mass media--Juvenile literature. | Epidemics--History--Juvenile literature. | Diseases and history--Juvenile literature. | Medical archaeology--Juvenile literature

Classification: DDC 614.5--dc23

TABLE OF CONTENTS

Many journalists took precautions such as wearing face masks while reporting during the COVID-19 pandemic.

Chapter 1

READ ALL ABOUT IT

In 2020, the world experienced the worst pandemic in generations. Tens of millions of people fell ill with a new disease called COVID-19. Businesses shut down as people were ordered to stay home to slow the disease's spread. By the end of 2020, more than 1.8 million people worldwide had died from COVID-19.

During the COVID-19 pandemic, many people stayed updated by watching, reading, and listening to news media. Types of media include television, newspapers, books, radio, social media sites, and more. In times of crisis, it is the media's job to keep people informed and aware.

Through news media, medical experts shared important knowledge about COVID-19. Leaders issued instructions and provided reassurance to citizens. Media also provided comfort and escape during the pandemic. As COVID-19 cases rose and closures persisted, social media allowed people around the world to remain connected.

In early 2020, members of the White House Coronavirus Task Force gave regular COVID-19 updates to reporters.

The COVID-19 pandemic was one of the first pandemics to happen in a world connected by digital media. But it was far from the first deadly pandemic to affect the world. In 1918, a new influenza virus infected hundreds of millions of people. As in 2020, media played an important role in shaping people's responses to the crisis.

Media Bias

Media is a powerful tool to educate and inform the public. However, during the 1918 and COVID-19 pandemics, biased media sometimes caused harm and confusion. Media is biased when it is influenced by a specific goal or opinion. Bias can affect what a news outlet chooses to cover. It can also affect how a news outlet covers a story. In 1918, for example, many US newspapers downplayed the severity of the pandemic. Instead, newspapers focused on the country's role in World War I to increase public support for the war effort.

To some extent, bias is an unavoidable part of media. Each reporter has a unique opinion of the world. In addition, different news outlets sometimes disagree about which stories are most important to cover. Despite these challenges, reputable media outlets try to be as objective as possible when reporting stories.

To successfully manage an outbreak of disease, health experts agree that communication to the public must be clear, unified, and accurate. Biased or false media can damage public health or divide opinion

SPANISH INFLUENZA--A NEW NAME FOR AN OLD FAMILIAR DISEASE

Simply the Same Old Grip That Has Swept Over the World Time and Again. The Last Epidemic in the United States Was in 1889-90

ORIGIN OF THE DISEASE

Spanish Influenza which appeared in Spain in May, has swept over the world in numerous epidemics as far back as history runs. Hippocrates refers to an epidemic in 412 B. C., which is regarded by many to have been influenza. Every century has had its attacks. Beginning with 1831, this country has had five epidemics, the last in 1889-90.

THE SYMPTOMS

Grip, or influenza as it is now called, usually begins with a chill followed by aching, feverishness and sometimes nausea and dizziness and a general feeling of weakness and depression. The temperature is from 100 to 104, and the fever usually lasts from three to five days. The germs attack the mucous membrane, or lining of the air passages—nose, throat, and bronchial tubes—there is usually a hard cough, especially bad at night, often times a sore throat or tonsils, and frequently all the appearances of a sever

around the neck as the heat of the body liberates the ingredients in the form of vapors. These vapors, inhaled with each breath, carry the medication directly to the parts affected. At the same time, VapoRub is absorbed through and stimulates the skin, attracting the blood to the surface, and thus aids in relieving the congestion within.

NO OCCASION FOR PANIC

There is no occasion for panic—influenza or grip has a very low percentage of fatalities—not over one death out of every four hundred cases, according to the N. C. Board of Health. The chief danger lies in complications arising, attacking principally patients in a run down condition—those who don't go to bed soon enough, or those who get up too early.

HOW TO AVOID TH E DISEASE

Evidence seems to prove that this is a germ disease, spread principally by human contact, chiefly through cough

In late 1918, some newspapers ran article-like advertisements that falsely claimed the pandemic influenza was no worse than the normal flu.

In large cities, newsboys sold newspapers to passersby on the street.

in harmful ways. In 2020, for example, misinformation about the pandemic was able to spread quickly on social media. This led to people disagreeing about how serious the pandemic was and the proper precautions to take.

Media in 1918

In 1918, media in the United States was very different than in 2020. In 2020, people could quickly access information, news, and entertainment on television, the internet, social media platforms, and more. But in 1918, people largely relied on print newspapers to stay up to date. Many cities had daily newspapers. Some published both morning and evening editions. In each edition, journalists updated stories with new developments.

In 1918, newspapers were the most trusted sources of news. But they did not always publish truthful and accurate stories. Newspaper publishers aimed to sell as many newspapers as possible to make a profit. This meant headlines and front-page stories were often exaggerated to attract attention. But during the pandemic, newspapers remained unusually quiet about the disease outbreak.

THEN VS. TODAY

In 1918, radios were mostly used by hobbyists to communicate over large distances. The first radio news broadcast occurred in 1920, one year after the influenza pandemic ended. By 2019, there were more than 15,000 commercial radio stations broadcasting across the United States.

A radio from the 1920s

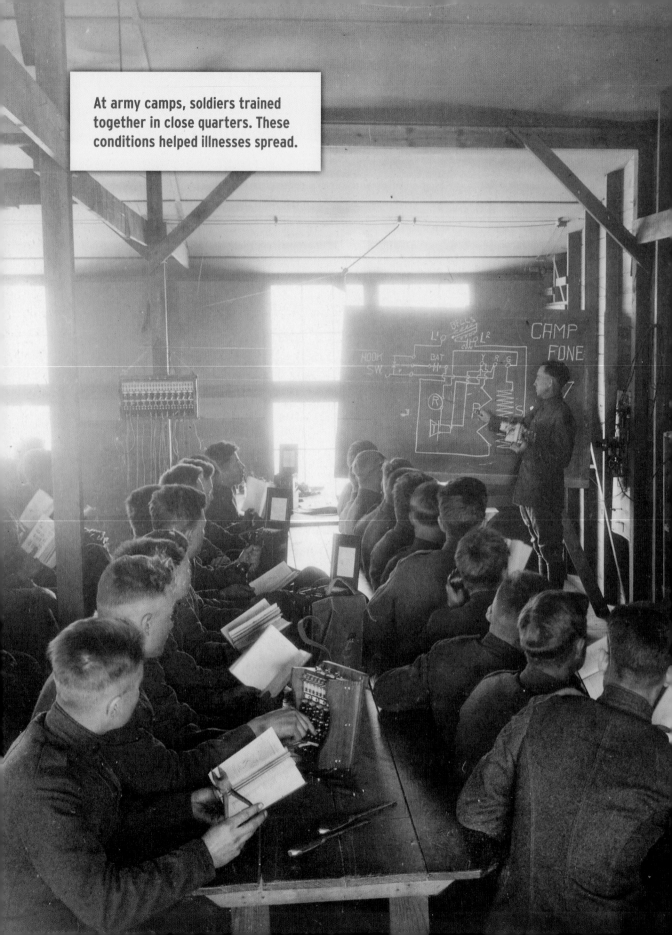

At army camps, soldiers trained together in close quarters. These conditions helped illnesses spread.

Chapter 2

A WARTIME PANDEMIC

In March 1918, US troops at Camp Funston, an army training camp in Kansas, became infected with the first known cases of pandemic influenza. The disease caused symptoms such as fever, runny nose, and sore throat. By the end of the month, about 1,100 of the camp's roughly 54,000 soldiers had been hospitalized with the virus, and 38 had died.

Although the influenza was infectious, most doctors were not yet concerned about its effects. Yearly influenza outbreaks regularly infect millions of people around the world. At the time, the illness affecting soldiers in Kansas seemed no more deadly than typical influenza.

The Committee on Public Information

When the influenza pandemic began in March 1918, the United States was fighting in World War I. The war had started in 1914. The United States had joined in April 1917. Many Americans

Journalist George Creel was appointed by President Wilson to run the CPI.

had not wanted to join the war. So, government officials wanted to convince the public to support the war. That way, people would donate time and money to the war effort. To this end, President Woodrow Wilson created the Committee for Public Information (CPI) on April 13, 1917. The CPI was responsible for producing positive stories about the war. The department created announcements, articles, advertisements, and other propaganda that were biased to portray the war in a positive light. Newspapers nationwide were encouraged to publish the CPI's materials.

Four-Minute Men

The CPI also employed approximately 75,000 public speakers called four-minute men, named for the short speeches they gave about the war in public spaces such as movie theaters, churches, and parks. The CPI encouraged four-minute men to create a sense of fear with the stories they told. In their speeches, four-minute men often portrayed enemy soldiers as less than human. Officials believed that fear of the enemy would help unite Americans in support of the war.

In April 1918, movie star Douglas Fairbanks promoted the war effort before a large crowd in New York City.

The Virus Spreads

As the CPI promoted the war, influenza cases continued to rise. By May 1918, tens of thousands of US soldiers were traveling around the world each month to join the fighting. The soldiers carried the influenza virus with them overseas. Troop movements helped the virus spread to millions of soldiers and civilians in the United States and other countries. This first wave of influenza subsided in the late summer and early fall. But a deadlier wave of influenza was just around the corner.

The Battle of Cantigny was the first major American battle of World War I. It was fought on May 28, 1918, in France.

Camp Devens housed tens of thousands of US troops in training.

As the influenza virus spread, it also changed. This is called mutating. When a virus mutates, it can become more infectious and more deadly. By August 1918, the same virus that had affected people in spring was deadlier than before. Several cases of this deadlier flu were first reported in soldiers in Boston, Massachusetts, on August 27. The virus soon spread to Camp Devens, a nearby army camp.

Around 14,000 people at Camp Devens caught the influenza virus over the month of September. Many people experienced normal flu symptoms. But some people suffered painful headaches or earaches. Others bled from the nose, mouth, or ears. And some people became sick with pneumonia caused by the flu. Pneumonia is an infection that inflames the lungs. Patients who caught pneumonia typically died. By the end of September, 757 people at Camp Devens had died of influenza.

The Second Wave

During September, Camp Devens faced growing numbers of influenza patients. As patients filled the camp's hospital, various staff, troops, and civilians traveled to and from the camp on normal business. This travel helped the virus spread. Within weeks, influenza had spread to cities throughout the United States. The second wave had begun.

As the influenza virus spread across the United States, the US Public Health Service (PHS) issued advice and warnings to the American people. The PHS was a government department. It received money from the US Congress to help promote the health and well-being of the nation. During the war, the PHS's duties involved protecting the health of US troops.

US surgeon general Rupert Blue headed the PHS. In October, Blue ordered the PHS to print 6 million pamphlets about the influenza. The pamphlets were then mailed to the American public.

TREASURY DEPARTMENT
UNITED STATES PUBLIC HEALTH SERVICE

INFLUENZA

Spread by Droplets sprayed from Nose and Throat

Cover each COUGH and SNEEZE with handkerchief.

Spread by contact.

AVOID CROWDS.

If possible, WALK TO WORK.

Do not spit on floor or sidewalk.

Do not use common drinking cups and common towels.

Avoid excessive fatigue.

If taken ill, go to bed and send for a doctor.

The above applies also to colds, bronchitis, pneumonia, and tuberculosis.

An October 1918 pamphlet issued by the PHS

Each pamphlet included information about influenza symptoms and gave advice on how to stay safe and healthy. The PHS also printed and distributed posters to cities across the country. These posters displayed information to help the public understand the dangers of influenza.

Unproven Cures

Pamphlets and posters helped educate some people about influenza. But not everyone could access the information. At the time, much of the US population lived in isolated rural areas. It was harder for PHS information to reach these communities. In addition, about 6 percent of US adults were unable to read.

Without access to sound medical advice, some people turned to unproven cures to prevent and treat influenza. Some people stuffed salt up their noses to stop the disease. Others wore pouches of garlic around their necks. One woman in Pennsylvania served onions with every meal. She claimed this protected her eight children from influenza.

In 1918, spraying medicine in the throat was thought to prevent influenza. But this was not an effective treatment.

Surgeon General Blue spoke out against false influenza cures. He reminded people that a cure for influenza had not yet been found. He also warned that unproven cures could do more harm than good.

No Distractions

While the PHS tried to educate the public about influenza, many media sources avoided discussing the crisis. Government officials worried that the pandemic would distract people from the war and lower the nation's morale. So, they insisted that newspapers downplay the danger of the virus by not publishing stories about it.

On May 16, 1918, Congress had passed the Sedition Act. The act made it illegal to say anything that could harm the United States or the war effort. During the pandemic, the law affected how journalists wrote about the influenza crisis.

On September 27, the Wisconsin newspaper *Jefferson County Union* wrote an article warning the local community about the flu. Using the

The CPI published pamphlets to encourage the sale of war bonds.

Rupert Blue earned a medical degree from the University of Maryland in 1892. He then joined the US Public Health Service (PHS) as an intern. Later, he was hired as an assistant surgeon in the organization. In this role, Blue battled several disease outbreaks across the country.

Blue was the surgeon general of the United States from 1912 to 1920. As surgeon general, Blue believed that the US federal government should provide more support for public health. He advocated that the government create a national health insurance to help care for American citizens. Once the 1918 pandemic ended, Blue also fought for a larger, more centralized PHS. He argued that the federal government should lead the public health response in times of crisis.

Sedition Act, a US Army general sued the paper for publishing the article. The general argued that the article had lowered the nation's morale and thereby damaged the war effort. Incidents like this worried other newspaper editors. It could take a lot of money, resources, and time to fight lawsuits in court. So, newspapers often avoided publishing

Blue was the fourth US surgeon general.

articles about the flu to be safe. As influenza case numbers rose, newspapers continued to publish the CPI's upbeat war stories instead.

Many Americans noticed a divide between what they were seeing and what they were reading. In major cities, tens of thousands of people were becoming sick with influenza each day. But newspapers barely reported on the illnesses. This caused some people to feel stressed and confused about whether to take the pandemic seriously.

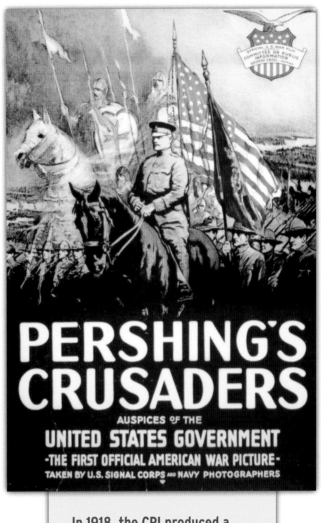

In 1918, the CPI produced a documentary about the US war effort. The film was advertised in many newspapers and shown across the country.

Morale vs. Health

Government officials often disagreed with the advice of public health officials during the pandemic. In Pittsburgh, Pennsylvania, the mayor told citizens to ignore warnings and advice from the PHS. In Philadelphia, Pennsylvania, government officials organized a large parade to raise money for the war. Health officials advised the government to cancel the parade. But on September 28, 1918, the Liberty Loan Parade brought hundreds of thousands of Philadelphia citizens to the streets.

The Liberty Loan Parade is now considered a super-spreader event. Super-spreader events involve large gatherings of people. As people interact, a disease can quickly spread from one person to many other people. The week after the Liberty Loan Parade, 45,000 people in Philadelphia fell ill with influenza.

The Pandemic Ends

In October 1918, the influenza virus killed 195,000 Americans. Case numbers remained high in November but declined by the end of the year. Starting in January 1919, the United States experienced a third wave of influenza. Although deadlier than the first wave, the third wave was not as deadly as the second.

By the summer of 1919, many people had

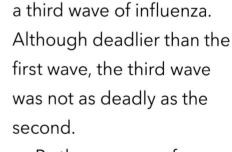

In April 1918, Philadelphia held a public boxing match to promote and raise money for the war.

World War I ended on November 11, 1918, during the second wave of the pandemic.

either died from the disease or recovered and become immune. When someone is immune to a disease, it means they cannot be reinfected. With less of the population to infect, the virus stopped spreading and became extinct. Worldwide, influenza had infected an estimated 500 million people, killing 50 million.

Very few people talked about or recorded their experiences of the 1918 pandemic after it ended. Modern historians believe that Americans were devastated after losing their loved ones to the disease and to World War I. So, many people simply wanted to return to normal life. As a result, the 1918 pandemic was largely forgotten by future generations.

In 2020, about one in five US adults got news mostly from social media.

Chapter 3

MEDIA EVOLUTION

In 1918, media mostly consisted of local newspapers. People had to wait for news to reach them. But by 2020, people could get their news from tens of thousands of different sources across a variety of platforms. Media technologies evolved for many decades to reach this point.

Television

In the United States, televisions first became popular in the 1950s. By the end of the decade, around 530 television stations broadcasted news and entertainment.

In 1957, a new influenza virus triggered another pandemic. Over the next year, the influenza killed as many as 1.3 million people worldwide. Televised news programs allowed people to stay informed about the pandemic. On November 2, 1957, ABC Television aired a news program about the virus, produced by Johns Hopkins University in Baltimore, Maryland. On the program, epidemiologist

Police officers and firefighters are vaccinated against the 1957 influenza virus.

Dr. Charlotte Silverman explained where the virus had come from and how to avoid catching it.

Internet and Social Media

In 1989, British computer scientist Tim Berners-Lee invented the World Wide Web. This information system is the foundation of the modern-day internet. Over the next decades, the internet grew to contain thousands of news websites. The rise of the internet also led to the rise of social media sites such as Facebook and Twitter. On social media, users could quickly share news and entertainment they found important.

From April 2009 to April 2010, a novel influenza virus sickened tens of millions of people worldwide. It caused a disease nicknamed swine flu. The internet helped build public knowledge about the virus. As news of the pandemic broke in April 2009, many people began posting about it on social media. This online talk drove people to search for further information online. In just one week of April 2009, for example, online traffic to the Centers for Disease Control and Prevention (CDC) website increased by 442 percent.

Plans and Preparations

US health organizations worked to prepare for future pandemics. Planning an internet and social media response was particularly important. By 2018, about 76 percent of adults preferred reading news online. That same year, more Americans got news from social media than newspapers for the first time in history.

Organizations such as the CDC planned how to quickly develop informative materials, such as infographics, during a new pandemic. These materials could be easily shared on government social media accounts. Health experts also concluded that government secrecy had weakened the US response to the 1918 pandemic. Experts from the CDC stated that media during a health crisis should be as open and honest as possible.

PANDEMICS BY THE NUMBERS

The COVID-19 pandemic caused many US adults to use social media more than before. In early May 2020, one survey found that 51 percent of all respondents were using social media more often than they had been before the pandemic began.

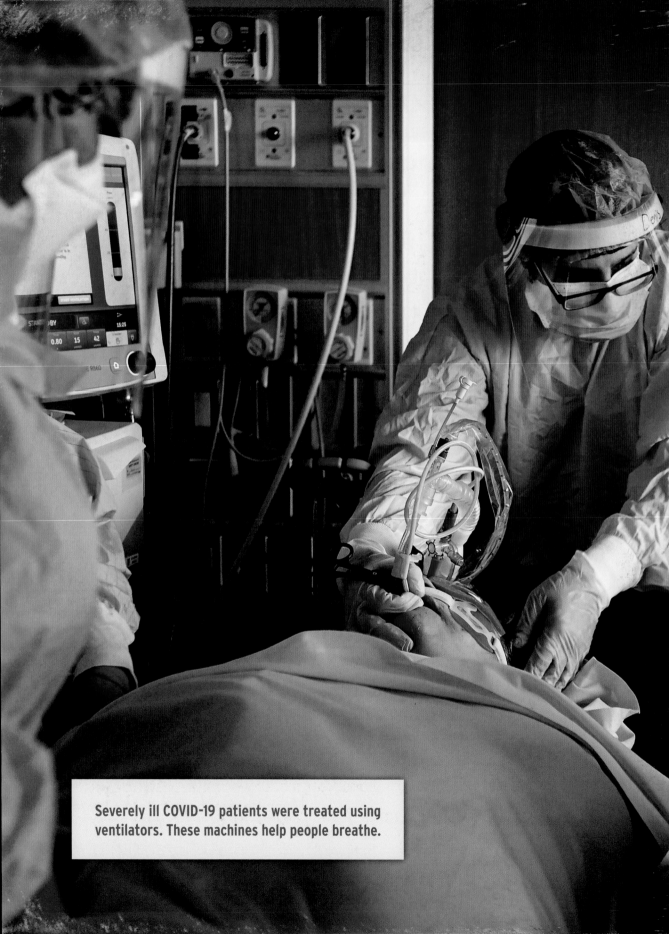

Severely ill COVID-19 patients were treated using ventilators. These machines help people breathe.

Chapter 4

COVID-19 STRIKES

In 2019, another deadly pandemic struck the world. In late December, several people in Wuhan, China, became sick with a respiratory illness caused by an unknown virus. On December 29, health officials from Wuhan's Center for Disease Control visited Wuhan Central Hospital, where several cases of the new illness had been reported. The health officials took samples from sick patients. Then, scientists worked to study the virus.

The virus was soon identified as a novel coronavirus. Scientists named the new virus SARS-CoV-2. The respiratory disease it caused was later named COVID-19.

Coronaviruses typically cause mild illnesses such as the common cold. Indeed, many people with COVID-19 experienced cold-like symptoms such as a fever and cough. But a small percentage of those infected suffered severe respiratory problems. Some patients struggled to breathe as they fought the infection.

Like influenza viruses, SARS-CoV-2 spread via respiratory droplets. When an infected person sneezed or coughed, nearby people could breathe in the droplets. Some people could even carry and pass on the virus without ever feeling sick.

Coronaviruses are named for the crown-like spikes on their surfaces. *Corona* comes from the Latin word for *crown*.

State Media

By the end of December, Chinese officials had reported the COVID-19 outbreak to the World Health Organization (WHO). However, the Chinese government did not announce any news about the virus to the Chinese public until mid-January 2020. Many of China's largest news outlets are controlled or influenced by the government. Because of this, the news outlets do not typically report on news that portrays China in a bad light. So, for weeks, China's government and media suppressed news of the disease.

The Whistleblower

As COVID-19 spread throughout Wuhan, several doctors who tried to share news about the disease were called liars by state media. Li Wenliang worked as a doctor at Wuhan Central Hospital. In December 2019, he became concerned by the growing numbers of

Weibo is one of the most popular social media apps in China. It has hundreds of millions of regular users.

patients suffering from the strange respiratory illness. So, on December 30, Wenliang sent a message to his friends using the Chinese social media app Weibo. He warned that a new disease was infecting patients. He also advised people to warn their families and friends about the disease. This warning was reposted by another account. Within days, it spread throughout Weibo.

In early January, Wenliang was held by police and accused of spreading lies on Weibo. Wenliang had to sign a statement admitting to this crime before he could return to work at the hospital. After returning to work, Wenliang fell ill with COVID-19. He died

Mourners in Hong Kong attend a vigil for Dr. Li Wenliang.

in early February 2020. Chinese citizens were angry about his death. Many saw Wenliang as a hero for trying to speak out about the virus while Chinese media outlets avoided reporting on it.

Officials later said they did not want to cause panic until they were sure the virus was a threat. Critics argued that informing the public about the outbreak as early as possible would have helped slow the virus's spread.

Beyond China

On January 13, the first COVID-19 case was reported outside China, in Thailand. Later that month, cases were also reported in Japan, South Korea, and the United States. By January 31, dozens of countries outside of China had reported cases. That day, the US government declared COVID-19 a public health emergency.

Many world leaders issued nationwide orders to slow the spread of the virus. Under these orders, people were asked to only leave their homes for essential travel, such as

Maryland governor Larry Hogan was one of several state leaders who gave regular press briefings during the pandemic.

The Johns Hopkins Coronavirus Resource Center tracked worldwide COVID-19 cases and deaths on its website.

buying groceries or going to the doctor. In addition, nonessential businesses such as gyms and movie theaters had to close. In late March and early April, many US governors issued similar statewide rules, called stay-at-home orders.

US Media

As the pandemic unfolded, more people in the United States began to read, watch, and listen to news media. Some television networks saw their viewership increase by almost 30 percent! Pandemic coverage consumed the nation's news.

News outlets kept people informed about stay-at-home orders. They also aired live press conferences from government officials. Some news sites built COVID-19 maps where people could track the number of COVID-19 cases in their state or county. And, many news outlets broadcast the stories of frontline health professionals working in crowded hospitals.

PANDEMICS BY THE NUMBERS

From March 16 to March 22, 2020, an average of 1.55 million viewers watched the news network CNN throughout the day. This was a 151 percent increase in viewership compared to the same time in March 2019.

Global Media

By March, most countries had reported COVID-19 cases. On March 11, the WHO declared COVID-19 a pandemic. Organizations such as the WHO and the CDC issued information about the disease. This helped communities around the world stay informed.

In early February, the WHO began holding regular press conferences about the coronavirus. Conference transcripts were posted on the WHO's website. In the conferences, health experts informed the global community about precautions to take against COVID-19. On April 6, the WHO recommended that people wear face masks to help prevent the spread of the virus. Face masks help contain respiratory droplets that can spread COVID-19. The WHO also explained how COVID-19 spread and when a person infected with COVID-19 was most contagious.

Many health organizations did their best to provide accurate, science-based information during the pandemic. Many news outlets in the United States and around the world helped distribute this information to the public. But not all news sources were reliable. With so much information available, it was sometimes difficult for people to tell which information was accurate and unbiased.

The CDC's Emergency Operations Center worked with the WHO to coordinate COVID-19 resources and information.

Some people protested pandemic restrictions, calling the pandemic "fake news."

Chapter 5

COVID-19 INFODEMIC

By the end of 2020, the United States had experienced three surges in COVID-19 cases. The first surge occurred in the spring and largely affected New York City. The second case surge occurred in the summer. Case numbers rose quickly in southern states such as Arizona and Florida. Up to 70,000 new cases were reported across the country each day. A third surge occurred in the fall and winter of 2020. By mid-December, the United States was recording almost 200,000 new cases each day. Hospitalizations and deaths also increased in most states across the country.

There were many online and off-line news sources to choose from during the pandemic. However, some of these sources published information that was not backed by fact or science. It was sometimes difficult for people to tell which information was correct. Some experts called this information overload an "infodemic."

Misinformation Hurts

More than 83 million people worldwide had fallen ill with COVID-19 by the end of 2020. In the United States alone, nearly 346,000 people had died. People across the world were worried for their loved ones. Many people were desperate to hear good news about cures or vaccines.

Disreputable websites preyed on people's hopes and fears by publishing false news stories about COVID-19. Some articles wrongly stated that breathing in steam or washing your nose with salt water would kill the virus. Other websites sold fake COVID-19 medicines to make money. One website told people that consuming tiny flakes of silver could cure COVID-19. In reality, these did not cure the disease.

This medical misinformation was harmful to public health. Sometimes, fake cures hurt people. Other times, individuals with COVID-19 took unproven treatments instead of seeking medical help for the disease.

In Bolivia, some street vendors sold a dangerous bleach-like substance as a COVID-19 cure.

Social Media Steps Up

On social media, people could share inaccurate information with their followers quickly and easily. This allowed fake news to spread. Identifying and blocking misinformation was an important part of stopping the COVID-19 infodemic.

During the pandemic, social media platforms such as Twitter and Facebook worked to reduce the spread of misinformation on their sites. In May 2020, Twitter made it harder for users to see tweets that displayed unofficial information about COVID-19. Tweets that conflicted with expert medical advice were blurred and marked with warnings. Users had to acknowledge the warnings before reading the tweets. Twitter also helped direct users looking for

Facebook's oversight board was co-chaired by Jamal Greene (*left*), a professor at Columbia Law School in New York.

information about the virus toward reliable news sources. For example, links to the CDC's website were displayed prominently in people's news feeds.

Facebook added labels to false or misleading articles, photos, and videos. The labels explained why the content had been marked false. People who tried to share labeled posts received pop-up warnings that the content was inaccurate. In October 2020, Facebook also launched an oversight board. The 40-member board included lawyers and human rights advocates. Facebook users flagged posts they believed were inaccurate. Then, board members reviewed the posts to decide whether they were truthful and safe. The board could then vote to remove harmful content.

Not everyone supported social media's effort to combat misinformation. Some people felt that Facebook and Twitter were violating users' free speech rights by removing and obscuring posts. Others believed it was beyond the scope of the platforms to label information as true or false.

Fact-Checking

As the pandemic wore on, public health officials constantly learned more about COVID-19. Because information changed so quickly, trusted news sources sometimes mistakenly published inaccurate or old information. In March 2020, the Trusted News Initiative (TNI) announced plans to create a universal fact-checking system for media companies. The TNI was founded in 2019. Its goal is to protect people from false news and harmful online content.

TNI worked with news sources such as the *Financial Times* and tech companies including Google to build a shared alert system. If one company identified false information on its site, the company alerted other members. Then, similar incorrect information could be quickly removed or updated across multiple sites.

Political Bias

The year 2020 was dominated by the COVID-19 pandemic. But in the United States, 2020 was also the year of a presidential election. Former Democratic vice president Joe Biden challenged sitting president Donald Trump for the presidency. The pandemic was a key issue in the election. Critics of President Trump accused the

Joe Biden often wore a face mask while on the campaign trail.

US government of responding poorly to the pandemic. Trump supporters accused Biden of not caring enough about businesses that were struggling because of widespread closures.

People's political biases often influenced how they felt about the pandemic. For example, Republicans were more likely to believe that COVID-19 was not a threat. They were also less likely to wear face masks, even though medical experts said this measure slowed the disease's spread. Democrats were more likely to support stay-at-home orders, even if it meant businesses across the country had to close. People often watch news media that is biased toward their political opinions. In 2020, many news outlets reported on the pandemic in ways that confirmed the political biases of viewers. Differing political views made it difficult for people to agree on the right way to respond to the pandemic.

Many people used video apps such as Zoom to hold virtual gatherings.

Sharing Is Caring

Media sometimes confused and divided people during the pandemic. However, media also kept people connected through the crisis. In many

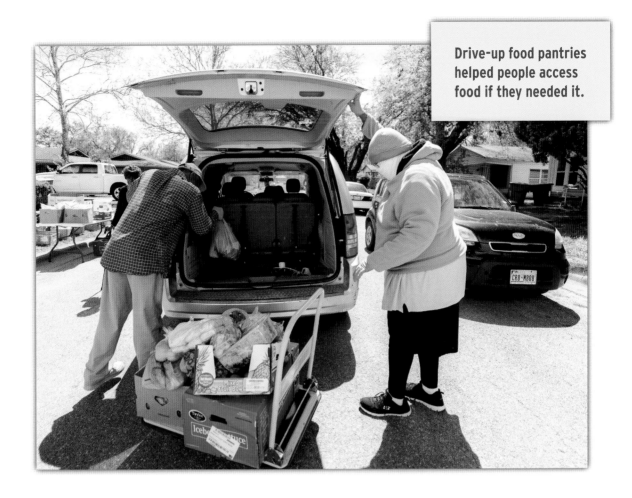

Drive-up food pantries helped people access food if they needed it.

countries, leaders told people to stay home and avoid nonessential travel during the pandemic. This meant people could not see their friends or visit their loved ones.

Many people suffered from boredom and loneliness because of these restrictions. But social media sites allowed people to stay connected virtually when they couldn't be together physically.

Social media also helped people connect with and help their neighbors. Some people were at higher risk of developing COVID-19 complications. These included elderly people and those with certain health conditions. For high-risk individuals, everyday tasks such as going to the grocery store could prove dangerous.

On March 18, the social media platform Nextdoor launched the Help Map. The Help Map was an interactive map of a person's neighborhood. People who were able to help their neighbors with grocery shopping and other tasks during the pandemic could add themselves to the map. Then, people in the area who needed help could look at the map and reach out to volunteers.

New Solutions

Media played an important role in connecting and informing people during the COVID-19 pandemic. The COVID-19 pandemic

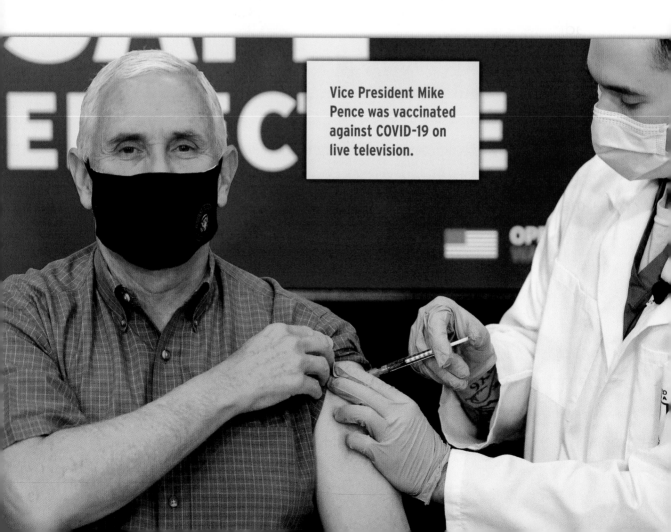

Vice President Mike Pence was vaccinated against COVID-19 on live television.

also helped countries learn the importance of communicating essential information to the public.

In December 2020, two COVID-19 vaccines from drug companies Pfizer and Moderna were approved for emergency use in the United States. By April 2021, the nation was administering more than 2.8 million vaccine doses per day on average. Health experts believed most US adults would be able to receive a vaccine by summer 2021.

ONLINE ACCESS

News publications such as the *New York Times* and the *Wall Street Journal* offer subscriptions. Customers who pay for a subscription gain access to news articles and other media. During the pandemic, these publications and many others made articles about COVID-19 free to read. This allowed everyone to have access to reliable health news regardless of their ability to pay.

As the end of the pandemic slowly came into view, people stayed connected by the shared experience of the crisis. The media landscape of 2020 had sometimes left people confused. But global media also helped people around the world understand and tackle the dangers of the virus together. In the future, the world would remember that during a pandemic, media matters.

TIMELINE

APRIL 1917
The United States
joins World War I.

APRIL 13, 1917
President Woodrow Wilson approves
the creation of the Committee
for Public Information (CPI).

1917

1918

MARCH 1918
Several cases of influenza are reported at
an army camp in Kansas. These cases mark
the start of the pandemic's first wave.

1989
The World Wide Web
is invented. It forms
the basis of the
modern-day internet.

1989

2019

DECEMBER 2019
China's CDC reports
a new, unidentified
disease to the World
Health Organization
(WHO). The disease is
later named COVID-19.

AUGUST 27, 1918
Soldiers in Boston, Massachusetts, become sick with a mutated strain of influenza. This strain causes the pandemic's second wave.

SEPTEMBER 28, 1918
The Liberty Loan Parade is held in Philadelphia, Pennsylvania. The widely attended event is followed by a spike in influenza cases.

**LATE MARCH–
EARLY APRIL 2020**
Many US governors issue statewide stay-at-home orders. As COVID-19 cases increase, more Americans begin watching news coverage of the pandemic.

APRIL 2021
The United States is administering more than 2.8 million COVID-19 vaccine doses per day on average.

JANUARY 31, 2020
The US government declares COVID-19 a public health emergency.

MARCH 11, 2020
The WHO declares COVID-19 a pandemic.

DECEMBER 2020
Two COVID-19 vaccines are approved for emergency use in the United States.

GLOSSARY

Centers for Disease Control and Prevention (CDC)—the main national health organization in the United States. The CDC works to control the spread of disease and maintain and improve public health in the United States and other countries.

civilian—a person who is not an active member of the military.

commercial—having to do with business or making money.

disreputable—not respected or trusted. Something that is respected and trusted by most people is reputable.

droplet—a tiny drop of liquid.

epidemiologist—someone who studies how diseases spread.

immune—incapable of being affected by a disease.

infographic—a chart or illustration that uses visual elements to present information.

isolated—separated from others.

lawsuit—a case held before a court.

misinformation—information that is untrue or inaccurate.

morale—the enthusiasm and loyalty a person or group feels about a task or job.

novel—new and different from what has previously been known.

objective—based on fact rather than opinion.

outbreak—a sudden increase in the occurrence of illness.

oversight—the act of overseeing or supervising something.

propaganda—media made and distributed to aggressively promote or damage a cause or group.

respiratory—having to do with the system of organs involved with breathing.

sedition–saying, writing, or doing something that encourages people to disobey their government.

sue–to bring legal action against a person or an organization.

surgeon general–the head medical officer of a branch of the military or public health service.

transcript–a written, printed, or typed copy.

World Health Organization (WHO)–an agency of the United Nations that works to maintain and improve the health of people around the world.

World War I–from 1914 to 1918, fought in Europe. Great Britain, France, Russia, the United States, and their allies were on one side. Germany, Austria-Hungary, and their allies were on the other side.

ONLINE RESOURCES

Booklinks
NONFICTION NETWORK
FREE! ONLINE NONFICTION RESOURCES

To learn more about pandemic media, please visit **abdobooklinks.com** or scan this QR code. These links are routinely monitored and updated to provide the most current information available.

INDEX